AF485681

In order to protect the privacy of the people that have submitted stories some names and locations have been left out.

All stories were originally submitted by our audience to ghostsofamerica.com. The stories have been edited by us to better fit this book.

Compiled and edited by: Nina Lautner

Acknowledgements

We would like to thank all those who have submitted their stories to us. These are the people who make our site ghostsofamerica.com and this book possible.

We would also like to thank all the lost souls in these stories. We hope many of them will have found their way by the time this book is published.

CONTENTS

31. Sharing The House - Longwood, Florida
32. The Man In The closet - Bradenton, Florida
33. The House Across The Church - Lagrange, Georgia
34. Demon On Grady Street - Thomson, Georgia
35. So Evil - Thomasville, Georgia
36. Karma - Thomasville, Georgia
37. In The House - Rock Hill, South Carolina
38. Disturbed - Darlington, South Carolina
39. The Yankee - Laurens, South Carolina
40. Just A Skull - Landrum, South Carolina
41. Small House With Full Basement - Huntsville, Arkansas
42. Old Nursing Home - Mountain Home, Arkansas
43. A House on 7th Street - Fernandina Beach, Florida
44. No One Saw Her - Saint Augustine, Florida
45. Rush of Air - Olive Branch, Mississippi
46. Cursed - Fort Payne, Alabama
47. Strong Stale Cigarette Smell - Mount Dora, Florida
48. Vanished - Okeechobee, Florida
49. It Didn't Want Us To Leave - Atkins, Arkansas
50. Feel The Vibration - Marietta, Georgia
51. A Lot Of History - Fort Benning, Georgia
52. I Have Seen A Ghost - Gainesville, Georgia
53. Lake Buckhorn Mystery - Temple, Georgia
54. Something Dark - Hattiesburg, Mississippi
55. Marching Towards The Cemetery - Andersonville, GA
56. An Old Nursing Home - Vidalia, Georgia
57. Two Inches From The Ceiling - Thomaston, Georgia
58. The Judge's House - Rome, Georgia
59. Child Like Entity - Rome, Georgia
60. Unwelcoming Vibe - Belleview, Florida
61. Last Room On The Left - Lake Charles, Louisiana

1.

In The Attic

Fort Myers, Florida

About ten years ago I spent the night at a friend's house in Dean Park. His grandparents had bought this old house and were gone for the weekend, so he decided to have a party. He told us all this story about how it was built by a judge that went crazy after turning his attic into an office and killed his wife and kids in the house. The woman that lived there before his grandparents bought the property apparently went completely gray from the stress of apparitions in the home.

There were stories of the shower curtain opening around the clawfoot bathtub while in use and cats always being uneasy when they were inside. I thought it was just a bunch of BS to scare us. I even volunteered to sleep in the office upstairs that used to be the "infamous" attic. My friends woke me up in the morning to see if I wanted anything from the store. I asked them to bring me back a coffee and went back to sleep.

As soon as they left I felt like someone was still in the room with me. I sat up slightly and saw a woman sitting at the desk with her back toward me. She was very thin and had brown hair and a red dress. I thought that maybe my friend's grandparents had come home early, and since I had never met them I thought it would be less awkward if I just went back to sleep and waited to be introduced later.

I went back to sleep. I waited until my friends woke me up with coffee. I told him that I think his grandma was home, and he looked at me like I was crazy. I explained what I saw, and he wasn't surprised. I never went back to the house until recently. I now live two blocks away from it and never realized until I was walking my dogs and recognized it immediately. I'm half tempted to knock on the door and ask the owners if they have experienced anything strange.

Submitted by Jeanette, Fort Myers, Florida
. . . .

2.
Chasing Shadow
Clayton, Georgia

There is an old two-story house that has been there since before the Civil War. It served many purposes according to the people who owned it several years ago. The house was supposed to be a school, a courthouse, a boarding house, and a family home. The stories the family told seemed fantastic. When I was a kid we visited the family, and I started having my own experiences.

One Friday night we were all sitting on the porch, and the kids decided to play tag in the dark. We ran around the yard for an hour or so. The other kids were tagged and made it back to the porch. I was chasing a person around the yard and a tree, and that was when I got yelled at by my mom. They saw me chasing a shadow but never able to catch it. Then my mom told me the other kids were on the porch and asked who I was chasing. I stopped and ran to the porch. They all told the story of me chasing a shadow around the yard.

One night we were all sitting in the "living room" of their house. (The place was set up like an apartment building at this time.) We were sitting, and we all saw a shadow in their master bedroom and go into the bathroom. The light came on, and the door shut. We noted how weird that was. We looked around the room and noticed families were seated in the room. No one was missing, so no one should have been in the bathroom. After ten minutes I was volunteered to go check it out. As I approached the bathroom, I could see the light was still on. I opened the door, and no one was there. I ran back to my seat, and the family said it was probably "the ghosts". They just laughed.

The next story is more ominous than the previous. I was staying with the family just before going to college. I was staying in a room upstairs. The upstairs is laid out like a hotel with several interior doors leading to a common hall. The hall was lit by a single light with a pull string to turn it on. There was a window at the end of the hall about 8-10 feet tall.

One night I went upstairs to go to bed. I could hear everyone downstairs laughing. As I reached the top of the stairs, I turned right to face down the hall. I took a step and then saw a dark silhouette in the hall near the string. I almost froze but got brave or stupid. I figured one of their sons was messing with me. I stepped to the side, and the shadow did the same. I stepped to the other side, and the shadow did the same.

I stood back in the middle and told them I didn't think it was funny. I reached the string and pulled it expecting to see their son. The light came on, and I was alone in the hall. I was unnerved at that point. I went to my room and pulled the covers over my head.

(That always helps.) More stories from that house, but some other time.

Submitted by Sid, Clayton, Georgia

. . . .

3.

Something Sinister
Irmo, South Carolina

I work for a house cleaning company, and my coworker and I were assigned a house in Friars Gate. It was vacant, and someone was getting ready to move in. We arrived and made our way inside. Nothing seemed too out of the ordinary. I took the upstairs. My coworker, let's call her Eliza, took the downstairs. I was cleaning in a bedroom up there and opened the closet to clean inside. On the inside of the door were spots of blood. It freaked me out, and I called Eliza to come look. She was freaked too. I wiped it off, closed the door, and made my way into the bathroom

As I was scrubbing the shower walls, I heard someone walking across the living room downstairs. I figured it was Eliza getting the vacuum, but then I remembered that I had it up here with me. I was puzzled, so I called her name. There was no answer. I went downstairs to ask if she was in the living room. She was all the way on the other side in the master bath. I went and asked her if it was her. She answered no and that she thought it was me. It obviously wasn't. That was the beginning of the horror.

I went out into the living room and heard a giant bang upstairs. I flipped. I thought it'd be best if we stick together. She helped me get my stuff from upstairs to bring it down. The air suddenly felt dark and heavy. We were both freaked. Once downstairs, I started working in one of the bathrooms. Eliza was dusting in the hallway. She stopped and had a strange look on her face. I asked what was wrong. "Did you hear that"? Was her reply. I said no, and she went on to explain that she heard a voice but couldn't make out what it said. I was starting to get more scared by the minute. I felt like something was watching. Then I heard it. It was a faint jumble of unintelligible words. It was nonsense. I was shaken.

Then I heard a series of bangs that sounded like car doors closing followed by a bunch of voices. We looked at each other in terror as we ran to the windows. No one was outside. We tried to hold it together as I started in the kitchen, and she went upstairs to the bathroom where it all began. I kept hearing a series of things that made me turn around to look behind me. All I saw were shadows darting out of my line of vision and then disappearing. Suddenly, I heard a loud crack in the living room. I dashed in, and Elizabeth came running down the stairs, supplies in town. "Eff this. We're out of here," she yelled. I kept asking what was wrong, and she finally told me.

Apparently she was dusting the blinds up in the bathroom and the toilet flushed by itself behind her. I agreed that enough was enough. We both could feel darkness closing in on us as we raced out of the house.

As I was putting our things by my car, I heard a distressed yell from inside the house. We threw our stuff in, and for a split second as I was getting ready to floor it out of there, I saw what looked like a tall white figure in the window. It must've been around nine or ten feet tall. Needless to say, we booked it out and refuse to ever go back.

I found out from Eliza on the way to the office that she felt like she was being watched by something sinister. She also saw the darting shadows and just felt terrified to her core. Someone has to go back to clean it the following day. I hope they don't have the same experience.

Submitted by Mas, Irmo, South Carolina

. . . .

4.
Not My Sister
Oldsmar, Florida

Back in 2012 I used to attend Keystone United Methodist Church on Race Track Road. My family and I would always get there a lot earlier than the service actually started because my dad was in the praise band, so they would practice early mornings. I would set up snacks and make coffee for the people attending the service. My two younger sisters at the time (8 and 10 years old) weren't allowed in the church kitchen.

One day I was preparing the coffee, and in the corner of my eye I saw a little girl run past me and into the pantry. Assuming it was one of my younger sisters, I called out that telling them they weren't allowed to be in there. When I got no response I went to go check the pantry, but the pantry was locked, and both my sisters were playing outside the church. Nobody else was around or in the kitchen at the time. The only other people in the church were my father, his band mates (all of which were on stage practicing at the time) and my mother who was outside with my sisters.

I was a little spooked, but considering the church building has its own cemetery I wasn't too surprised. The girl might have followed me home, however. The next night as I was explaining my sighting to a friend, and I saw a little girl run past my glass front door.

There was no one outside. I never saw her again though. That wasn't my first spirit interaction either, but that's a whole other story.

Submitted by AE, Oldsmar, Florida

. . . .

5.
He Died In The Kitchen
New Smyrna Beach, Florida

My children and I lived in a house on Old Mission that was comprised of two train cars put together forming the 'shell' of the house with the house being built over it. It was a shotgun-style house setup and kind of cool. However, from the first week of our move in I did not like or feel at ease in the kitchen. It honestly gave me a sense of dread, which was really weird since to me it's the heart of a home. I never ever felt that way before.

I thought "well, I'll clean it top to bottom and set it up, and then I'll feel better about it." Nope. Didn't work. I lit a white candle and did a cleansing, prayerful intention. It felt better for a day or two. Then again I felt ominous. We also had a dog who was blind, and when we'd be sitting in the living room she'd go to this one particular spot and bark repeatedly with her back fur standing up. She would always be looking up towards the ceiling. That unnerved us, but we got used to it.

Now the (one) bathroom was at the very back of the house next to the kitchen and my teenage daughter's room. My daughter later told me that if she would wake in the night needing to pee, she would hold it until morning because she didn't like the kitchen and bathroom at night, even with a nightlight on in each room. It was months before she admitted that she felt like she was being 'watched' by something in the kitchen.

Six months into living at this house, my next door neighbor walked over to officially introduce himself, and he and I stood on the kitchen side of the house. The last window down was the kitchen window. He pointed to it and then told me the father of the former tenants had dropped and died of a heart attack in the kitchen. You could have knocked me over with a feather! It all made sense like pieces of a puzzle coming together. The hair stood up on the back of my neck. I've always been what is known as a "sensitive," and as the years have passed by, my daughter has much of the ability too (although she hasn't tapped into it like I do.) We both knew something was wrong and 'off' with that kitchen. And yes, I do believe our (blind) dog sensed and felt his spirit. We only lived there for one year and that was long enough.

Submitted by Jen, New Smyrna Beach, Florida

. . . .

6.
The House On Smokey Road
Newnan, Georgia

It's gone now, the house on Smokey Road. I can imagine why. Never in my life have I experienced anything like the events in that house and property. To this day, 30 years later, I do not drive past it. I am not sure I should write about it. Suffice to say, someone at church was talking about a weird house they heard about near Newnan. Overhearing the conversation my son butted in and said "you must be talking about the house on Smokey Road. " The woman looked startled and said "well, yes I was. " My son remarked we lived there for about a year and a half before we got the hell out.

No one who ever walked into that house was not impacted; sooner or later by experiences in the house or on the property or when they went home. My kids saw things and experienced things, so did their friends. I never could sleep in the big downstairs bedroom in the 120-year-old house. It was cold. Even with no air conditioning the room always felt cold. I started sleeping in what we used as the family room between the living room and the big foyer and hallway that led to living room. I started hearing things and sounds that were so loud they woke me up.

We heard sounds like banging and someone throwing boxes and large items in what would have been the crawl spaces between the upstairs bedrooms. First I thought it was critters. It must be some big critters for the noise they made. I would go up and check and nothing would be disturbed. After awhile I got used to it. I would roll over and went back to sleep. My children then about 12, 16 and 18 all had bone chilling experiences. My daughter would wake up at night, and the window would be rattling so hard she thought it would break. It felt and sounded like wind, but no wind was blowing.

The worst experience was the "thing" that she saw in the corner. It was a greenish gnome like character staring at her. One night she sat up in bed to see her big brother who was attending Georgia Tech at the time, standing between her and the "thing. " He was wearing a Tech sweatshirt. She yelled his name and asked "what are you doing here?" The figure disappeared. When he came home to visit he told about a dream he had a week or so before that he was home and in his sister's room, and something was behind him as he tried to call to his sister.

Before he found himself back in his bedroom at Tech. Things went bump in the night. Electricity bills were through the roof even though I did not use a lot of electricity. We had no computers at the time, no washer and drying hooked up or a gas stove yet. The following months we had electric bills in the hundreds of dollars. On one occasion my daughter had a sleep over birthday party. Several of the guests said in middle of night they wanted to go home because something was watching them and breathing on them.

A friend of mine came over one day when I was not home. The door was unlocked, so she came in. She heard music coming from upstairs, the song Lemon Tree by Harry Belafonte was playing, and she heard arguing. It was a loud argument between my daughter and my ex-husband. She felt she was intruding but called out. No one answered, so she went upstairs, and no one was there.

Two weeks later my daughter told me she had gotten into an argument with her dad, and the song Lemon Tree was playing at the time. So many things happened there. We would see a figure at the window when we would leave. We had cold spots and a feeling that something horrifically bad had happened there - murder or something. After it became clear something was wrong with the place, we gave notice and moved away. When we talk about it now, we all agree those things did happen. We did not imagine it, and someone who moved into the place found it so malevolent they bulldozed it and built a brand new house on the property. It was near a bridge, where some young people had crashed their car, even though no other cars had been in the area.

As far as I am concerned the entire area is cursed or something. I was told the surrounding 100 square miles had been part of a very large plantation before the Civil War and that Voodoo had taken place. I believe that. When digging for a foundation in that area I came across carved figures, old pipes, and kind of stones and fetishes I have not seen before. The area is haunted or it's got some kind of bad energy. Whatever it is, I am glad we moved out. Nothing like it ever happened again. My kids grew up, but they still talk about the house on Smokey Road.

Submitted by Diane, Newnan, Georgia

. . . .

7.
The Chef
Helen, Georgia

I was around nine years old when this happened. My mom, my cousins, and I took a drive to Helen. When we got there it was 1 am. Since it was late at night there was no one to be seen, and all stores were closed, so we kept driving around. We slowed down in one of the streets. We could see that there was a man with a chef outfit on outside smoking. I kept staring as I had just awoken from a nap. We all started to talk about how weird the man looked as we passed by. It was as if he were lost.

We kept driving with the purpose of making a turn and going back to check out the shop where the man was standing in front of. We kept driving, and we came along a small walking bridge. As we slowly drove past it, my mom and my cousin both claimed to have seen a large group of people walking across it.

I quickly turned around to look at the bridge, but the street was lonesome. We kept driving, and we came to the same turn where we believed the man was standing earlier. We approached the shop. When we got closer we realized that the shop had all the lights turned off, and the door was boarded up. We found it strange since we had been on the same road just a few minutes ago. Since then I have never gone back to Helen that late at night.

Submitted by Anonymous, Helen, Georgia

. . . .

8.
A Steven Steam Victim
Graniteville, South Carolina

This was a hitchhiker experience I had in front of Steven Steam. She was a middle aged thin black lady who was still pretty. I was driving in Graniteville passing the Steven Steam Plant when I saw her. I stopped. She got in and directed me where to drop her off. The exact moment she closed the door she vanished. It wasn't "right before my eyes." I turned the car around and realized the house she said was hers was abandoned. She was nowhere, and the door was a decent distance from my car, so I would have seen her go in the house when I turned around.

This was in March in 2005, after the Graniteville train wreck, so I am convinced that she was either one of the Steven Steam victims, (though I don't recall a female victim in Steven Steam Plant) or she was outdoors during the train wreck and died that way. Either way I am convinced she was a ghost. She wasn't glowy, transparent, or creepy in any way.

Submitted by Sierra, Graniteville, South Carolina

. . . .

9.
A Grey Shimmery Man
Rock Hill, South Carolina

The Victorian house on East Main Street has been razed some 40-odd years, but memories of the various activities manifested therein live on. In the back yard was a cemented pond that had fish that no doubt attracted the very young child who slipped, fell in, and died circa 1920s. For the next forty years a child was seen running through the home's back porch, especially during the bad electrical storms Rock Hill used to have with great frequency in the summer.

Knockings heard here and there weren't the sounds of an old house settling; they always came in threes and mostly downstairs near a back stairwell and the adjacent hallway and rooms. When the home's upstairs rooms were used as a boarding house, one of the roomers literally dropped dead as he was halfway up the stairs in the late 60s. He could be heard previously in his room making noises such as walking heavily and kicking off his work boots. His noisemaking restarted a few weeks after his passing. The room was locked.

After two times going in and finding no living soul there, the proprietors just kept the room vacant and locked. Noises continued in that room infrequently until the house was vacated in 1976. There was another strange thing or two at the house next door, the corner house. Unoccupied during the 60s and 70s, the old place called the Ratteree House would have a window light up briefly, or a lesser light would pop up in a window then disappear. This was before the time of security lights and timing devices and, anyway, the lights were there only for a brief moment and had no apparent pattern. No telling how many times they appeared as the house wasn't exactly under surveillance.

In the back yard of the house was an enormous stump. It was at least nine feet in diameter to my recollection and was about four feet high. Unexplained knocking noises could be heard from the unoccupied property, and they ceased when crossing through the bushes to see what was going on.

It wasn't like woodpecker rapid fire rat a tats. They were stronger chops and had a moment's pause between them. They sometimes lasted for a few minutes to about an hour, but never happened when someone was present and watching the area around the stump, the apparent source of the noises.

However, early one morning the head of the house, hearing the sounds, went to investigate and swore to his deathbed that as the stump came into view, the sound stopped. Then he saw standing beside it a "grey shimmery man" with a hatchet immobile, then fading away as he watched. I've never seen a spirit, but this man believed he did. I believe him; he was my father.

Submitted by Anonymous, Rock Hill, South Carolina

. . . .

10.
Sinful
Mobile, Alabama

I must have inherited some strange DNA from my Mother. She spent her teenage years with an aunt who lived on St. Charles Avenue in New Orleans. In those days there was no TV, so people spent their time calling up spirits and having séances. While at the Richards Home and Museum (DAR House) upstairs and looking out a window, a very strange foreboding feeling came over me.

Soon after the tour guide told of a ghost that was known to stand in front of and look out that very same window. Weeks later while at the public library I was pulled like a magnet over to a bookshelf where my hand randomly removed a book about ghosts of Mobile. Sure enough the story of that ghost was in the book. It frightened me, so I swore to never return to that house because spirits have been known to follow you home. My late mother had also instructed me as a child that delving into the spirit world was a very sinful thing to do.

Submitted by Bob, Mobile, Alabama

. . . .

11.
Loud Knock
Gulf Shores, Alabama

My family stays on the Ft. Morgan peninsula every year. In 2008 during Hurricane Ike a shipwreck was uncovered near our house. There were seven of us staying there including a baby and a toddler. One evening as the storm was passing through the Gulf headed west the electricity would go off for a short while and then would come on again. The toddler was sitting at the kitchen bar drawing and coloring, and he was humming a childish little tune.

A couple of us heard a strange disembodied voice harmonizing with him. Harmonizing! We were incredulous, but he didn't appear to have noticed. The next evening the storm had passed, and the skies were clear, but the wind and surf were still high. During dinner we heard a loud knock down low near the floor on the utility room door from inside the house. After checking the room (we already knew there was nobody there) we found it empty.

Another year when I was staying at the house alone, and there was nobody else even staying at any of the nearby houses. I faintly heard a woman's voice coming from a middle room of the house. I charged in there and firmly told whatever it was that I had no plans to share the house with them and that they should immediately leave. I guess they did because since that night there hasn't been anything else creepy going on.

Submitted by Coco, Gulf Shores, Alabama

. . . .

12.
My Daughter's Friend
Lonoke, Arkansas

I lived in a home on Dismukes and felt things there. My daughter was two or three at the time, and I knew she could see things we felt or couldn't see. She would talk about a bad man. Outside one day I saw an old lady in a nightgown standing behind my husband. We left that place soon after.

The next place wasn't much better. We lived in a trailer on Maple Street, and there I saw things. I saw this little girl about my daughter's age and height. My daughter was four or five at that time. I saw her out the corner of my eye, and I started talking to her like she was my kid. She went into the room that was my daughter's, so I got up off the couch and asked her why she didn't answer me back. She said "I've been in my room playing. I haven't left. I was OK". She said that the little girl I saw was her friend and they play together. We also had a dark shadow that stayed in a corner of the living room. I felt really bad about that. I could feel its negative energy. The place we live at now has no problems.

Submitted by Amber, Lonoke, Arkansas

. . . .

13.
They Are In Our Woods
Sanderson, Florida

Well, I can tell you that Sanderson is haunted. We had two ghost sightings in one week back in 2016. We live right near the Osceola National Forest, and my in-laws have lived here for years. My sister-in-law's have always said they have heard horses walking outside their bedroom windows when they were little. Let me remind you that right in front of our houses was the main dirt road the soldiers would use to get to the Olustee Battlefield.

One night my son Dylen was walking back to our house after seeing his papa next door. I was standing in my bedroom, and I could see him just standing in the living room not saying anything looking scared. I asked what was wrong. He whispered twice "mom, come here," motioning his hand to come to him. I said "what is it?" in a panic. He told me when he started to walk outside of his papa's house he could hear horses near the house. We have no horses around our house. Then he said when he got half way he saw an apparition hovering over our deck. He was so panicked and was saying "oh my gosh" with his hands on his head.

I was a little freaked out that night, but then two nights later my son Dalton and his friend had come home around 12:00 in the morning. I was up talking to them about their night. My son Dylen had taken out our dog to walk. He then came back into the house and went into his bedroom. Probably thirty minutes had passed, and I was sitting on one end of the couch with the sliding glass door behind me. Dalton was sitting on the other end. Dalton was talking to me. Then all of a sudden his eyes started looking at something behind me. I started thinking about what Dylen had seen just a few nights before this night, and I threw my hands over my ears and started to say "what what what?" I knew he was seeing something behind me. He asked "Is Dylen outside?" I screamed "no. " He threw his hands over his eyes and slammed his body back onto the couch. I could not move.

Dalton sat back up with tears in his eyes and said he saw a young man in a white shirt walking and looking straight ahead of him. Then it stopped and looked at him. He said as soon as their eyes met he disappeared. He said that he could see him but could see through him. I could not go to sleep that night, and I kept replaying Dalton's scared expression. I don't think none of us that were there that night will ever forget that. Both of my sons back then were 17 and 19, so to see my big boys scared like that I know ghost are real, and they are here in our woods.

Submitted by Malissa, Sanderson, Florida
. . . .

14.
The Mysteries Of Archer Spirits
Archer, Florida

I am a born and raised Archer resident with ties to the city for over 42 years. My parents have lived in the same home for 42 years, and it was purchased in 1977. I don't know much about the home prior to my parents purchasing it.

My whole life something never felt completely comfortable about the home we lived in. I've had many experiences in the home that shook me to my core. Most recent was Thanksgiving week 2018. As a child, I was awoken one night from a dead sleep. There was no light in my bedroom other than the light from an outside utility light post that was shining in the window.

From the outside light I could see a dark silhouette of a figure standing at the foot of my bed. There were no facial features that I could see. It was only a dark cape and top hat like a magician would wear. The figure then raised his arms, and my bed started to rise. Immediately I was terrified. What child wouldn't be scared out of their mind if this happened? I just closed my eyes real tight and refused to allow myself to see it. I told myself "nope, it's not there" and fell back asleep.

That was at least 30 years ago, and I still remember it like it was yesterday. I remember exactly how my room was decorated and set up. I remember the PJs I was wearing that night, every single detail. Other things like feelings of being watched and shadows from the corners of my eyes have happened. For many years as a child, I slept in my sibling's bedroom and refused to sleep in my room. As a child and young adult, I would always be fearful to go outside after dark. Literally I would avoid it at all costs. I hated it!

Most recent was during a visit for Thanksgiving. The morning we were leaving I was packing up the car at around 5:00 a.m. It was still very dark outside. I made several trips to and from the car and into the house without any thought of my fear of the outdoors at night. I mean it's been many years, and my mind has matured greatly. During a trip to the car I loaded some things into the car and was about to head back into the house when I heard a VERY LOUD scream. It was like a hackle, like a witch's hackle.

Now I've heard some animals before that make weird calls that can sometimes sound like a baby's cry or screams, but this was no animal. This made my adrenaline immediately peak. My heart literally dropped. It stopped me in my tracks. All the years living in Archer, I've never heard that sound before. It was not from animals or anything. I have never heard that type of scream ever in my life. Immediately I high tailed it into the house and let my hubby finish the packing. Once again the mysteries of Archer spirits continues to baffle me.

Submitted by Jennifer, Archer, Florida

. . . .

15.
At Base Lodging
Charleston Afb, South Carolina

I stayed at base lodging for a week while I was there for training. It was the second building just down the street from the main office. My room was on the first floor. There were two ceiling fans, one in the living room and one in the bedroom. Both controlled by two separate remotes. There were a couple of nights where the fan in the bedroom would turn on by itself and a couple of nights where the light on said fan would do the same. One of those nights I was lying in bed when the light turned on, I grabbed the remote and turned it off. The light kept turning on after each time I clicked the off button. It was as if something in there was playing with me. (It was quite annoying.) Finally, I said "please stop. I'm trying to sleep," and it stopped. I debunked the phenomenon by seeing if the two different remotes would turn on the fan and lights in the opposite room. I did this because I thought maybe the person in the next room over was inadvertently turning my light on. It wasn't. Pretty much every night I would hear weird noises coming from the bathroom. I never saw any apparitions, but I wouldn't be surprised if someone else has.

Submitted by Lauren, Charleston Afb, South Carolina

. . . .

16.
Do You Know Ally?
Maylene, Alabama

In 2012-2013 there was a ghost little girl that would appear in my home in Maylene on Brantley Lake Road. She would play and talk to my at that time 3-year-old daughter. She was amazed at my daughter's toys and loved to play with them with or without my daughter playing. I thought that my daughter just had an imaginary friend. One day I was washing dishes at the kitchen sink, and I felt someone beside me.

At first I thought it was my daughter standing beside me, but I heard her upstairs playing in her bedroom. When I turned to my left to see who was standing near me I saw a ghost little girl stand there with long blonde hair and a white long dress on. She was barefooted, and by the way she was dressed she looked to be from the 1800s. I talked to my daughter about her, and she told me her name was Ally.

One day my daughter ran downstairs screaming and said the man scared her. I asked her what man, and she said the man that appeared in her room and took Ally away. I believe he was Ally's father that came and got her. Many people in my home would see her in our home, sitting on stairs facing our living room. She would walk down the hallway and peek into the hallway from my daughter's bedroom. When her father came to get her and took her away we never saw her again.

I told my neighbor about her, and she said she had heard for years that back in the 1800s there was a woman with many children. She had them in the back of her horse and buggy. One day the mother hit a pothole, and the little girl about three years old fell out. The mother ran over her killing her. I have searched online trying to find this little girl's grave to find more information about her. I can't find it. I also looked at archives and old newspapers online to find her. I don't know if Ally is a nickname. It's hard to find her with not knowing her last name, dates of birth and death.

Submitted by Michelle, Maylene, Alabama

. . . .

17.
Tall Faceless Being
Fort Walton Beach, Florida

I grew up on Maples Street across from Gatlin Lumber. On several occasions a dark tall faceless being would come into my room but only as far as the door. I would call for daddy. He would say I was having a bad dream and would put me in bed with him and mama.

But one night as the creature came to my door I said softly daddy? And it took a step closer. Then I said daddy louder and it proceeded to come closer now right as it was looking down at me (it had no face) I screamed daddy!!! And daddy jumped up so fast that he slipped on the waxed terrazzo floors and cut his head open on the radiator.

We spent the rest of the night at the emergency room at Eglin. For years he told me it was a bad dream. But once I was grown up he told me he had seen it many times too. (He didn't want me to be scared) we moved not long after to what was once called Driftwood Estates and no more dark creatures.

Submitted by Anonymous, Fort Walton Beach, Florida

. . . .

18.
Could It Be Chester?
Sarasota, Florida

I grew up in a little house in Siesta Heights. As a very small child, I would notice a figure walking through the living room at night. You could only make out a dark figure and what appeared to be the glowing end of a cigarette in its hand. Every night it would walk around, ending at the doorway of my bedroom. I could see it standing there for what seemed like forever, before turning and going into my parents' room. This went on every night, for as long as I can remember. I always thought it was my dad, and it made me feel safe in the dark when I would watch this going on.

It wasn't till I was a teenager that I began to question this. Dad did smoke, but he was so afraid of falling asleep with a lit cigarette, that he would not smoke in the bedroom. He wouldn't even allow an ash tray in the bedrooms, so how was I seeing him take a lit cigarette every night into the bedroom and not coming back out? I shared a room with my sister, who was seven years older, until she went off to college. I asked her one day if she remembered someone watching us from our doorway at night. She laughed and said "oh, yes. Every night. " I asked her why she didn't say something about it, and she said she didn't think anyone would believe her. She too agreed that it couldn't have been dad because this figure always walked into our parents' bedroom with a lit cigarette and didn't come back out.

After dad had passed away in 1980 mom sold the house, and we moved back to Tennessee. I asked her if dad got up every night and smoked. She said that she was never aware of dad ever getting up at night, but no way would he enter the bedroom with a lit cigarette.

She told me about an imaginary friend that I had when I was little. I told her his name was Chester and that he lived in her closet. I would sit on the end of their bed and talk to Chester for long periods of time. I was sure that Chester was real, but they just assumed that I had heard that name on TV. Now I wonder. Strange things happened in that house. Could Chester have been a spirit? Could it have been him I saw walking around every night? I guess I'll never know.

Submitted by GLH, Sarasota, Florida

. . . .

19.
Not Allowed To Talk About It
Zephyrhills, Florida

My family bought a historical old home in Zephyrhills between the old Methodist church and what was back in 1967 the junior and senior high schools, both in one old brick building. We lived in that house on Tenth Street for almost fifty years. I grew up there. The first few years there was a creaky old screen back door, and the spring squealed and loudly slammed when used, much to my mom's annoyance. After a few years she finally nagged my dad into replacing it with a quieter solid door.

It was only one week later that while we were watching TV around 9:00 pm, we all four of us heard the unmistakable squeal and slam of that screen door. At first no one thought much of it since it was such a familiar noise. Footsteps could be heard crossing the wooden porch kitchen and dining room floors. My mom, my sister, and I were becoming quite scared as the footsteps got closer to the room we were in, especially when my usually lazy and calm dog began barking hysterically with hackles raised at nothing we could see.

My dad quickly turned off the TV, and in the following silence we distinctly heard the steps continue past us then up the stairs. The whole time my dog howled and rolled his eyes in terror. We all looked at each other in our own growing fear. My dad said sternly and a little shakingly, "that didn't happen. And never even speak of it: never. Clear?" His word was law, and so we never told anyone nor spoke to each other of it. Yet I for one could hear it many times through the years often late at night with the steps always ending outside my bedroom door.

Submitted by Sharona, Zephyrhills, Florida

. . . .

20.
They Are Roaming The Area
Comer, Georgia

The entire city of Comer burned to the ground in the late 1800s. Fire swept down the railroad tracks and consumed the wooden city, hotel, jail, and all. Shadowy figures can often be seen near a defunct railroad crossing, and a pair of young girls can sometimes be seen standing on the old water tower, though the structure is now too feeble to support a human (there were many times I scaled it as a child.)

One of my close childhood friends told me one morning of an incident from the night before; this was when he was about fifteen. He had awoken the night before, and gone to fetch a glass of water. Being a warm summer night in a small town, the front door had been left open, with the screen door closed. As he returned with his water, he saw a group of objects on the front step.

Slowly, three disembodied male heads rotated to look at him. They were grizzled and bearded, eyes burning like coals. Boy and specters looked at each other for several long seconds; then the heads rolled away down the steps and into the night. Not knowing what else to do, and with the creatures departed, he returned to bed.

Often while walking, particularly in the areas along the railroad tracks where graineries once stood, a sinister presence can be felt. Footsteps can be heard following you. The temperature may drop suddenly, and digital devices malfunction with surprising frequency.

Decay seems to take hold almost immediately. New structures appear to age at an accelerated rate. The entire town has an air of abandonment, though most of the homes and businesses downtown are occupied. This is due more to the persistent damp from a high water table than any supernatural force, but it creates an eerie atmosphere that feels ripe for paranormal activity.

The regular incidents of "ghost trains" certainly do not help dispel the feeling. The same geography that allowed the fire to sweep along the tracks results in the horns of trains many miles away to be heard at intervals. However, the mechanics of sound cannot account for the occasional glimpse of ancient flashing lights or the hiss of the steam engine you may encounter walking along the tracks on a foggy night.

My parents' land was home to a mule farm and logging operation, and many a night we could see the swaying lamps and hear the creaking wagons and thumping hooves of ghostly animals returning home from a long day's work.

The local graveyard is a hotbed of activity, though it is far from malicious. As children we used to cut through to get to the fairgrounds. Several times, while going through the graveyard or the downhill slope of woods that connected with our property, I remember stumbling and having an invisible hand shoot out to steady me.

I was recording video in the graveyard last year (not for spooky purposes.) This was a video project of walks through various towns and rural areas, and the graveyard was part of my loop through town. I had my dog that day. I kept feeling that I was being followed. My dog repeatedly gravitated to a pair of children's graves.

When I watched the video later, I was surprised to find voices that were not my own. The first, and the point when I went back to listen to the audio, is a child's voice saying "doggy" at the children's graves. This is followed by the sound of a young girl humming and singing, which persists for most of the remainder of the video. The other, which stands out in my mind, you can hear near the grave of a husband and wife a man's voice which says "I am happy. She is happy. We are happy together. "

Once, while walking in near dark along this hill, I turned around and ended up at the edge of a swamp. There was very little light, and I was unsure of how to get back to the path without becoming mired in the mud. I heard an animal walking toward me. It sounded like a large dog. Thinking it was one of our German Shepherds, I called to the dog. After a moment I felt it brush against my leg.

The dogs knew the command "home", and when I used it the dog immediately began walking. Though the brush was fairly heavy, we passed through easily. After several minutes we came to the bridge which leads to a path wide enough to drive on. I saw the shadow of the animal step onto the bridge before me. Then it melted into the darkness. I had been able to hear its feet crunching in the leaves, and the water below would have splashed had it jumped off.

When I returned to the house I found that the dogs had been inside since early that evening.

Many years later when I was married and had moved away, thinking nothing of the mysterious animal, I was visiting home and had been on a walk in the woods. When I came back to the house, I found my husband standing in the yard.

"Whose dog was that?" He asked.

"Dog? I hadn't seen any dog. "

"There was a black dog following you. "

I immediately thought of the incident in the woods, and suddenly realization dawned. It HAD been one of our dogs in the woods that night, our dear departed black lab cross who passed away before the German Shepherds were born. She is still roaming the woods she loved, keeping her family safe. Several times since I have heard people mention glimpsing a friendly black dog out of the corner of their eye, leading the way home.

Submitted by Ej, Comer, Georgia

. . . .

21.
Someone Else Was Not Pacing
Covington, Georgia

My husband and I bought our first house on Stacia Drive. In the three years we lived there a few strange things happened. The first was when I would go to work and set the house alarm. The sensors from the inside went off a few times, and nobody was home. I would get a call from the alarm company while I was at work to see if we were okay.

We had a wedding clock, and I noticed one day it wasn't working, so I knew I needed to change the batteries, but I didn't have any. About a week later my husband and I were getting ready to go out, and I noticed before we walked out of the house it was working and had the right time, so I thanked him for changing the batteries and fixing the time. He looked at me and said "I thought you changed it. I noticed it wasn't working a couple of days ago. " To this day we have no clue how that happened.

The house was a split level house, so when you walked in from the garage and passed the kitchen there were three or four steps up on the right to go to the two bedrooms, bathroom, and the master bedroom. Ten to twelve steps down to the left was another living space, a room, a bathroom, and laundry room. The master was upstairs all the way to the back.

The whole time we lived there we would hear footsteps pacing the hallway, and the footsteps would sometimes stop in front of the master bedroom door. My husband worked nights at the time, so I was super scared. I started having my lab sleep with me in my room, and I would lock the master door. Two years after we lived there my friend came to visit from Florida, and I never told her or anyone for that matter about the things we saw and heard.

I guess I was scared too until we sold it. Then I can open up about it. Anyhow, my friend was sleeping downstairs in our other living space. I was three months pregnant at the time, and the next morning she asked if I was okay. I said "yeah why?" She said I heard you pacing all night. Then I told her that we have been hearing that as well since we moved in.

We sold the house the following year, and up until recently I have been trying to find any history on the house and haven't been able to find anything. I remember the previous owners told us they had an above ground pool but set in in-ground.

Eventually they put everything pool related inside the pool and buried it all in the back yard. I sounded strange to us, and now we think maybe somebody drowned, or they just didn't want to deal with the maintenance of having a pool. I wish I would have asked. Anyhow, this was 1999-2002.

Submitted by Wondering, Covington, Georgia

. . . .

22.
Help Them Cross Over
Dalton, Georgia

In 2000 my family and I found an abandoned house outside of Dalton. We crossed some railroad tracks and drove down the drive way. Upon entering the atmosphere changed completely. It was as if it were frozen in time. There were brand new clothes from the twenties piled five to six feet high which still had tags on them.

One room had six iron twin-size beds. Upstairs was a room filled with fabric McCalls patterns and magazines. Across the hall was a room filled with astrology and witchcraft books. Down in the kitchen was a small table and one chair. Outside was a well and old smoke house.

However, it was the workshop behind the house that I experienced the most fear. Upon entering I got visions so clearly of a young black girl about twelve. She was begging for me and my daughter of about the same age to help her. It was as though she took over our minds, so that we could see and feel every horrible torture she had experienced.

My daughter took some of the books home with her, and crazy things started happening, so we took them back. My only regret is I can't remember how to get back there, and I want to return and help that girl and many others cross over, so they can finally rest in peace.

Submitted by Anonymous, Dalton, Georgia

. . . .

23.
Booger Building'
Fort Polk, Louisiana

I was a janitor, and we used to clean a building that was the old South Fort emergency room that is now being used for a child development center on Utah Avenue. I had always heard of the haunting there. They said a young boy (no more than seven years old) roamed the place in the evening. I did in fact encounter the little boy on several different occasions. He would knock over our brooms, open doors, and put hand prints on windows we just cleaned. They were just mischievous things a boy his age would typically do.

I saw him at the end of a spooky hallway one night, and around the same time letters on a bulletin board rearranged themselves to spell PARADOX! I felt like something was following me every time I worked in that building to the point that I refused to enter it alone. One night I was heading up the hallway because I had to get some extra cleaning supplies, and I saw the black figure that was childlike walk down the hallway towards me. It then went through the wall and out onto the playground equipment. That was enough for me to say out loud the crossing over ritual that was intended on safe cross over to the other side, and/or if it was Satan that it was compelled by the blood of Christ to leave us alone and do our job. I never saw the little boy again. Either he was crossed over, or he was Satan masquerading.

A year or so rolled by, and I was working another job coming home late one night. I decided to do a pass by the building, and lo and behold I saw a man-like figure looking out of the window almost as if to say there was a lot of paranormal activity going on in this building. I mean from what I know, it was a defunct hospital that may have even had a morgue in it. Literally many people came here to die. I have worked in several other buildings on the base, and I have never encountered anything as unsettling as that.

One of my co-workers even dubbed it the "booger-building" in reference to the paranormal activity that took place in that particular building. I was also temped through a telepathic brainwave mechanism to almost go down a corridor where the trauma patients were taken too. Talk about a tough mental fight with something that has rearranged letters to spell a message out (Paradox) and was trying to lead me down the corridor of advanced darkness. I never ventured down it. Eventually I left that occupation because of the intrusive thoughts that accompanied me when I worked in that building. My suggestion is that definitely be blessed up if you dare go to this building.

Submitted by Gordon, Fort Polk, Louisiana

. . . .

24.
I Was Pushed
Florence, South Carolina

One night some of my friends and I went to Montrose Cemetery. At the time I was five or six months pregnant. Well, when we got there everything felt normal, so we started walking around just looking, and we started hearing voices in a distance. My sister-in-law and I decided to walk back to the car. When she and I got to where the big stone wall was something came out of nowhere and pushed me from behind. It pushed me into my sister-in-law.

There was so much force that if my sister-in-law wouldn't have been standing I would have fallen on my stomach on a sharp stick that was standing up in the ground. It scared me to death because it felt like whatever it was didn't like the point that a pregnant girl was there. It felt evil, and I just felt like it really wanted to hurt me.

When we got back to the car I was shaking, so my friends and my boyfriend came to the car. My boyfriend said something made him drop his keys. When he bent down to pick up his keys he said he felt as if something was trying to pull him through the ground by his hand. Later all of us got in the car, and on the way down the dirt road which was also a hill we could see something jumping from one side to the other. It just stopped when we got completely down the hill.

Submitted by Jessica, Florence, South Carolina

. . . .

25.
Coffee Spilled
Madison, Alabama

In the mid 1970s I lived on Lanier Road in an apartment. One morning I was getting dressed for the day. I was in my bedroom putting on makeup in front of my dresser mirror. On the dresser was a small stereo with a speaker on each side of the mirror. I had a cup of coffee sitting in a saucer on top of one of the speakers, and the radio was playing softly. As I was putting on mascara, I saw out of the corner of my eye the coffee cup rise up out of the saucer and hover for a second or so. Then it sailed past me only to dash onto the bed behind me.

I stood there for a minute with the mascara still in my hand just staring at the now empty cup lying on the floor. Coffee spilled all over me and the bed. I looked in the mirror and saw where I had smeared mascara across one side of my face. I looked at my wet clothes and bed and the empty cup and ran to the front door. However, as I opened the door, I stopped and asked myself "what you're going to run out into the yard? Get back in there. This is your home. You have nowhere to go". I went back inside but moved away a couple of months later.

Submitted by Nonnie, Madison, Alabama

. . . .

26.
The Same Man
Semmes, Alabama

I maybe have a ghost story or maybe not. I just don't know, but I definitely have something to share. I can't explain what I have seen. I want to share and see if anyone has experienced this. Well, here it goes. The first time I saw this I was about nine or ten years old. I was with my step dad and my step uncle. We headed home one night from my other step uncle's house. We cut down this dirt road just off of Kali Oka Road in Mobile, Alabama, where there is an old plantation house with a structure that I understood was a slave home. Yes I know about the history of the plantation house, but at the time I did not know.

As we were headed down the road, a car came racing down the same road we were on and ran us off into an embankment. As soon as we hit the dirt embankment I turned to look at the car that caused us to wreck, it was gone just that fast. However, I did see a very slender and very tall black man about what look like eight feet tall crossing the road. He was staring right at me very calmly. It was as if he wanted me to know I could see him. As he crossed the road and stared at me he just went into the woods and into the darkness where I could no longer see him. That was the first time. The next time was in a different location off of Lot Road in the Georgetown area on my friend's parents' property.

Just behind my friend's home is a huge field, and we set up camp at the edge of the woods. We got the tent set up and the camp fire going. We were just being teenage boys and having fun hanging out. Well we all got ready to call it a night about 11 pm or 12 am in the morning, and we were getting ready to get some sleep. All of a sudden we heard what sounded like a woman screaming in the woods. Of course we thought it was a panther. We all froze from fear and were just scared to death to even make a breathing sound. We got our courage up and made a B line to the car and lock the doors. There were two in the front seat and two in the back seat.

I was sitting in the back seat on the driver side of the car. I was so sleepy that I could hardly keep my eye open. As I was starting to close my eyes and laying my head back on to the seat to go off to sleep, I saw from the rear view mirror the very same man figure as I did as a 9-or-10-year-old boy. He was tall enough to lean over the trunk. He looked right over the back car window right at us with no effort at all. I yelled to the driver of the car to crank up and go now, and without hesitation he did just that. As I looked back as we were driving off, he was the same tall and slender man. He looked right at me, and I could see it was the very same tall and slender black man, and he just vanished in the darkness.

That was my story, and on the two different locations was the same very tall and slender man. If you are from Mobile, Alabama and know the two areas and know who that man is or what this is, I would love to hear from you and your story.

Submitted by Charles, Semmes, Alabama

. . . .

27.
Looking At Me
Fayetteville, Arkansas

In 1998 I had moved to Arkansas by way of Eugene, Oregon. I can't remember the name of the brick apartments we lived in. However, one evening about an hour removed from turning in for the night, I was sitting on the couch, reflecting. I looked over toward the kitchen on my left, and I saw a girl ghost in a white gown with ratty unkempt hair. She was about ten years old with a distortedly large frown mouth - like when you stick your fingers in both corners of your mouth and pull down. Also, she had angry piercing eyes. She was carrying a baby doll, the kind teenagers practice motherhood with. She was just standing there, looking at me?

After I caught her gauze she slowly proceeded walking towards the couch on which I'd been sitting. This took about twenty seconds. I was scared frozen, until she reached the corner of the couch. At that juncture in time I was able to jump up and run out the front door of the apartment. She's the only ghost I've ever seen which I couldn't explain away with either research or elaborate rationale. It so happened the doll she'd been carrying was the same doll that my roommate's kid found upon moving in to that approximation of hell.

I was about 28 and would drink often and had an odd proclivity to hang the doll from the ceiling fan and then punch it, just to get a rise out of my roommate's daughter (things you do when you're stupid and drunk). I honestly still can't believe how real she was although she was somewhat transparent as well as how horrifying the mouth and eyes were to me. I wish I could say I had an imagination worthy enough to justify letting this go, but my imagination is as Mr. Rogers as they come, especially for it to be pulling of something so bizarre.

Submitted by Jason, Fayetteville, Arkansas

. . . .

28.
Giggling
Russellville, Arkansas

I used to live in a house on Pine Twist Lane outside of Russellville. I was blow drying my hair one morning, and when I turned off the blow dryer I heard little kids giggling behind me. No one was home but me. Another time my husband and I were downstairs cooking dinner, and I heard a bunch of people talking upstairs. I looked over at him to see if he heard it too. He did. We thought we had left a TV on upstairs, but we didn't. We couldn't understand what they were saying.

I would sometimes find things moved or rearranged in a different position. Every time we would have guest overnight they would ask us why we kept turning off the ceiling fan or TV. We never went upstairs when company was there.

I found out after asking neighbors there was a Civil War cemetery about 200 feet down the road. I couldn't find any history on the land anywhere, but there had never been another homestead on that land. Our house was only a year old. There was a Cherokee reservation that connected to the back of our property.

Submitted by Nicole, Russellville, Arkansas

. . . .

29.
Right Through Him
Cape Coral, Florida

I used to live in SE Cape just off Country Club. I was young when it happened probably around twelve, give or take a year. I was in the back seat of the family van as we were driving back from a get-together with friends around midnight. We were driving east on Veterans somewhere between Skyline and Santa Barbara.

We were in the right lane, and I don't think there were any other cars around. I was looking out the window, and I saw as the headlights shined upon a man dressed in old clothing. He stared wide eyed and with his mouth open blankly into the open road.

My first thought was that he was on drugs. He was walking almost zombie-like into the road as we approached. He then stepped over the white line right in front of our car. I closed my eyes to brace for impact as we headed straight for him. A few seconds later I opened my eyes astonished. We didn't hit anything.

We drove right through him, I thought. I didn't turn around, and I didn't say anything. I thought it was weird that nobody else in the car said anything about him and that my parents didn't swerve or change lanes or anything to avoid driving 50 miles an hour at the man in the road. I didn't ask my parents about it until a week later, but they had no recollection of him.

Submitted by Josh, Cape Coral, Florida

. . . .

30.
A Man On A Motorcycle
Miami Lakes, Florida

The encounter occurred in 1995 when I was twenty while driving back from the Edge nightclub in Fort Lauderdale. I was driving my old 79 Nova and must have been between 3-4 am. We were taking the usual backcountry route on I-75 less used stretch of highway back then. We saw a bright white light emitting all directions under the overpass bridge ahead for NW 154 Street (formally closed off bridge and road to the undeveloped west end back then.) Unable to make out what was in the center at first, I think the words my friend muttered were "what's that?" And no other words followed until after we passed it.

It helped tremendously that someone else shared the experience. It made it much easier to comprehend for us. I mean friends would believe us back then, but there's still a good deal of lingering doubt, so having that second person acknowledge and agree to the same story made it easier to comprehend.

As we got closer, something unusual came into view. It was an apparition of a man on a motorcycle (street bike.) He had on all the same color (blue violet) with true holographic mist, along with the bright white light emitting out. I didn't know whether to stop, pull over, or turn around. I didn't know what we were seeing. It seemed unaware of our presence as it remained motionless, pointing the opposite direction of lanes.

He was there just sitting on his motorcycle holding the steering column. Once I cleared it and it was behind us, we both yelled the typical "what was that?" We kept turning our heads around, and it was still there and continued to be visible until the next exit where by then I had mustered up the courage to take a closer look. By the time we turned back it was gone.

The area where this occurred is known as Maddon's Hammock, and it is adjacent to the locally known Tequesta Indian burial ground. Historically there has been a heavy presence of supernatural occurrences. Now the area has been almost entirely developed as residential homes, instead of a county park, an idea that was tossed around many years. Leaving speculation to what sort of activity homeowners living there have been experiencing.

Submitted by MESKK, Miami Lakes, Florida

. . . .

31.
Sharing The House
Longwood, Florida

We have lived in our house for twelve years, but our ghost just started acting up three years ago. When it all began my husband was out of town, and I had a large tree removed that morning. Our AC had also died that day. The dog was in the bed with me that night as we tried to stay cool with fans, and we were both awakened about 3:00 am with the loud sound of the TV on in the other room full blast. At first I thought someone had broken in, but the house was secure.

The following morning as I waited for the AC repair man, a stack of about seven books that had been sitting on a level end table for at least a month just randomly toppled over. At this point I was just thinking that it was some kind of coincidence. Then about two weeks later (again when I was home alone) I heard a sound that sounded like wrenching metal and a thud. The noise went on for several seconds. I found that our shoe rack in the garage had fallen. It was the sound of the rack falling because the screw fell out or something. The sound went on way too long for that. It was as if someone ripped it out of the wall.

Since then we have had lots of things go missing and turn up back in the first place you looked. There were lots of electronic oddities such as an alarm going off in the middle of the night using a ringtone other than the one you have selected. While I don't think our ghost is dangerous, he is rather annoying. I have had the most success in getting him to leave us alone by threatening him and yelling at him. I'm sure he'll act up again, but as long as he leaves us alone for the most part I'm okay sharing the house with him.

Submitted by Meghan, Longwood, Florida

. . . .

32.
The Man In The closet
Bradenton, Florida

The house I am writing about is on 11th Avenue NW in Bradenton. My family moved into it the year I was born. I always had a bad feeling at night in the bedroom I shared with my brother. He doesn't remember seeing anything, but he had the same feeling. I don't recall seeing anything either, but my sons do. My oldest who is nine now has had a few experiences though he can't remember them now. We were staying at the house when he was about three or four.

One day my wife was home with him and heard him playing in his room and talking as if he had a friend over. Knowing that he was in the room by himself, my wife went in to see what he was doing. She asked him who he was talking to. He told her he was playing with a little girl. He then went on to describe what she was wearing and how old she was. He also said that she told him there was a man who lived in the house that hurt her. Well, my wife being thoroughly creeped out tried to write it off as his imagination.

About a month had passed by when my son came out from his nap and said nonchalantly that there was a guy in his closet. He said the man said he liked to hurt little girls and that he'd hurt him too. Mind you this was all in the room I used to share with my brother. The one we both had a bad feeling about. Before all of this my wife always had a bad feeling when left alone or at night in the house. She's always been a bit more sensitive to these things than me. However, she's not the dramatic type, so I've always believed her.

Well, we are back at my parents' house, and now my two-year-old is sharing the room with my oldest son. Recently he's been screaming bloody murder when being put down for bed at night. He will continue to scream until we turn some kind of light on for him. He can't talk that well, so we can't ask him what's going on, but when he screams he faces the closet. Kind of creepy. We're trying to find out about the previous owner but can't find anything.

Submitted by Daniel, Bradenton, Florida

. . . .

33.
The House Across The Church
Lagrange, Georgia

When my girls were small we moved into a house on North Barnard Avenue across from the church. My oldest daughter was four and was afraid to use the toilet in the main bathroom. She kept saying there was a little boy in there. My husband and I thought she had a big imagination. A few months into living there we had occurrences with appliances turning themselves on, a flashlight turning itself on, and strange noises.

We ended up breaking our lease several months early. We were lying in bed one night about to fall asleep, and it felt like someone slapped the bottom of the bed. Thinking the fitted sheet must have popped off, we turned on the light to fix it, and the bedding was all still intact.

Years later my youngest daughter was invited to a sleepover at the same house. I asked the mother if they had experienced anything unusual. She just smiled, but the teenage son said that they had lights turn on and heard noises all the time. My daughter ended up calling me to pick her up before midnight that night.

Submitted by Laura, Lagrange, Georgia
. . . .

34.
Demon On Grady Street
Thomson, Georgia

In 2003 my family and I moved into the at the time blue and white apartments on Grady Street behind the movie theatre. We were told it was once a boarding house for the depot as well as the first McDuffie county jail. At the time I was five. I'd started getting visits from a solid black figure that would tell me to go down to the railroad tracks to play. He smelled like sulphur. I told my brothers and grandmother about it, and my grandmother told my mom.

My mom nailed all the windows shut. She brought a priest to bless the apartment. She also got holy water as well as sage, but nothing worked. She tried everything possible. On several occasions we'd hear something big with large nails crawling and scratching across the attic floor.

One Easter we all sat in the living room watching Passion of the Christ, and right when the devil started to scream a picture my mom had hanging up on a wall lifted up off the hail and flew off the wall nearly hitting my brother in the head. We all witnessed it. We then ended up moving down the road into the brown house at the stop sign.

My room's closet had the attic entry way in it. It was one that had a board you had to push up and move over. Well, we thought moving would make the entity leave me alone, but it didn't. It followed. Every morning my mom would have to come in and close the attic entry way because it would be open. Every single morning.

The thing still tainted me. The last time we saw it was one night when my mom and her boyfriend were sleeping in bed. She said she felt something hit her on her shoulder, so she quickly woke up and looked up to see a pitch black tall figure standing at the end of her bed. Usually when someone is standing on your bed there's an indentation, but there wasn't any. She said the thing leaned over in her face. She immediately said in a very forceful tone "in the name of Jesus, leave my house now!!" It then flew out the window causing the blinds to shake.

It was a demon. A demon was attached to me. I'm now 21, and I've had a few other situations happen, but nothing like what my family and I experienced on Grady Street in Thomson.

Submitted by Erin, Thomson, Georgia

. . . .

35.
So Evil
Thomasville, Georgia

I'm in my mid fifties now. When I was fifteen years old, my mother and I lived in Thomasville, Georgia for a few months. My mother worked downtown at a bar and grill as a grill cook. The owner's name was Jake, and his wife's name was Carla. He was completely scarred all over from a plane crash. He kind of terrified me by his appearance, but he was a nice person. My mother rented a big two-story house dirt cheap, and it was walking distance to her job downtown. We lived near the old oak tree that was hundreds of years old. We lived through pure terror in that house.

First we heard footsteps all night long upstairs and coming down the stairs. We would open the bedroom door, and we both stepped in to look at the stairs during footsteps. Nothing was there that we could see. We walked home one night down the sidewalk, and we saw the porch swing swinging wildly back and forth. There was no wind blowing. Some nights we were so scared. We would stay on the porch swinging all night because the noises inside of our rental house were out of control. We are not scaredy cat-type women or the nervous type, but this house was evil and terrifying.

Our screens were being cut also which scared us. The screens were fine when we first moved in, and we began noticing screens cut even as with a sharp knife. Luckily, we locked our windows. I also noticed all our neighbors were super unfriendly and avoided any contact with my mother and me. That was strange in itself. Eventually I found out through my own research at the Thomas County Library through old newspapers on microfilm. I went to the basement of library to research.

A gruesome unsolved murder had happened in that house about 1970. I found photos of the house we lived in in old newspaper articles about the murder. It was 1977 when we lived in the same house. An elderly woman was murdered and tortured horribly before her murder. I won't go into details, but it was horrible and gruesome. They did pick up a man from the mental institution and police claimed he killed her. I don't believe for one second he did it. I read the details, and nobody believed he killed her.

One of the things happening to this poor murdered lady was cut screens in the months before her murder. She had reported being stalked and harassed by something she never did see. Several of the things my mother and I had been terrified by. We moved immediately, and to this day I'm convinced she (her spirit) was trying to scare us out of that evil house before her murderer murdered us. He seemed to enjoy terrifying his victim for months before he murdered her. I believe my mother and I were next. I do not remember the address, but I remember what the house looked like clearly.

It is located just a few blocks from downtown Thomasville and a block or two from the ancient oak tree. I don't even know if it's still there. I hated that house as far as our horrific experiences there. The house was an old Victorian and so pretty but so evil. I believe her killer was alive, and we were next.

Submitted by Tonya, Thomasville, Georgia

. . . .

36.
Karma
Thomasville, Georgia

This happened in a big gray house on Clay Street. It was a two-story house that my grandmother, uncle, aunt, and two cousins lived in. I spent the night several times there, but I always slept in my grandmother's room since the house scared me. Several times I could hear a woman walking up the stairs in high heels. I could also hear a baby crying.

One time my uncle got up early, and he was drinking coffee in the kitchen when a man walked into the kitchen. The man poured himself a cup of coffee, and my uncle asked him who he was. The man disappeared, and the coffee cup dropped and broke.

One time my cousin and I were playing video games in his parents' room. My cousin went downstairs, and the door slammed shut. I thought my cousin was playing games on me, but he was still downstairs.

Years later sadly enough my cousin was shot and killed at a house a couple of blocks down. When my cousin died he appeared to me when I was in the army at the time in the boot camp. I called home and said "I know something is wrong". That was when I found out that my cousin died. He was only fourteen years old.

I remember when my late cousin was young one time he pointed a gun at my uncle, and he said he would kill him. At that point I knew later on in life my cousin would die. Karma came around and got him. To this day, I still experience hauntings no matter where I go. I don't like to call myself psychic, just intuitive. It's a curse and a blessing.

Submitted by Melissa, Thomasville, Georgia

. . . .

37.
In The House
Rock Hill, South Carolina

On White Street there used to be a house where a gruesome murder suicide had occurred in the 1940s. That house was torn down, and the site is now a driveway beside the Domino's location. Anytime there have been ghost investigations at that general site cold spots occur. At night orbs are seen, and no doubt EVPs could be captured if you're patient and had the right equipment. I've been there at night in the late 1990s, and it felt like there was a static electrical charge in the air but only there in the driveway.

Across the railroad tracks from there on Standard Street is a home, presently occupied. I won't give the house number. It is a home where in the late 1970s strange things such as unexplained noises and a general feeling of unease were present in a back bedroom. The sounds had a strange echo-like quality and came from one particular wall. There had been a death there in the 1960s in that room and maybe that entity just didn't want to move. I hope things have been more peaceful since.

Submitted by Anonymous, Rock Hill, South Carolina
. . . .

38.
Disturbed
Darlington, South Carolina

In Darlington County on a farm on April Drive near Mechanicsville there is a place where they recently cut down trees, and now there are brush piles and logs lying everywhere! When you go down the road you sometimes see someone in a white shirt or old looking clothing walk into the brush, but when you approached where they were there was no one there!

At first people thought it was someone living in there, and police were called. Water and food was left there never to be touched. This "person" has been seen by numerous people, including myself. He is always disappearing into nowhere and has been seen many times in May 2019.

It would be great if someone could come here and check it out. This is near very old farmland, and when they cut down the trees it is believed that they may have disturbed a grave or something there. This is not a joke and seems to be truly something weird. There are many stories of strange happenings in this same area.

Submitted by JC, Darlington, South Carolina

. . . .

39.
The Yankee
Laurens, South Carolina

My wife and I were visiting relatives in their circa 1912 home. I awoke in the upstairs bedroom in the large manor home believing my wife had turned her phone on, as a white flash of light pulled me from my slumber. To my left a man in what I now believe was a Civil War Cavalry uniform was standing, staring down towards me. I never felt threatened. He stood approximately 5'8"-5'9" tall and had deep creases in his sun-weathered face. His uniform was dusty. At first I thought it looked like a "Rough-Riders" uniform, similar to pictures I'd seen of Teddy Roosevelt in the San Juan Hill battle.

I gently elbowed my wife and calmly whispered, "There's a ghost in our room. " She raised her head and saw nothing. He was gone. She told me "Stop trying to scare me." I closed my eyes, and a minute later peered over to see him standing there again. I felt a heavy sadness in the room with him. I was excited to finally see an apparition. I'd worked with hospice for years and often heard stories from clients and patients near death of "seeing" deceased relatives or "spirits and ghosts" calling them.

The next morning at breakfast I reported my sighting. My wife's first cousin's husband is a minister. She entered the kitchen and said "Did you just say ghost? There was one in our room last night. I don't believe in ghosts, but I told him to get out, and he did." (I found that ironic.) She also reported she was not threatened by his presence but was uncomfortable being watched over by a stranger. Understandably.

This occurred three years ago. I recalled it and became curious recently because of a visit to Gettysburg, PA. I, as crazy as this may sound, believed since I was five years old that I was an officer who served with George Washington in Valley Forge. I was born in the Land of Lincoln, Illinois and married a Southern gal. I'm called "The Yankee," despite having lived in Virginia for over 48 years. True, fantasy, crazy imagination, who truly knows? But it makes life interesting, and I'm happy to have been included in the questions and speculations!

Submitted by Anonymous, Laurens, South Carolina

. . . .

40.
Just A Skull
Landrum, South Carolina

This happened to me in January 2017. I worked third shift at Amazon at the time. One night I got off work early, and instead of going to bed I decided to go for a walk through the woods. Where I live I don't have any neighbors just woods all around. I went out and the whole time I swear it sounded like I heard footsteps following me faintly through the woods. Every time I stopped they would stop almost right after. My first thought was it was an animal like a coyote or fox, but he didn't sound like a four-footed animal.

I was walking around, and I decided to make my way back to the house. I went through this large clearing and decided to squat down to see if I could see anything come out of the woods on the other side. When I squatted it down and listened it sounded just like someone came up to the edge of the woods on the other side of the clearing and then just stopped. I sat there for about ten or fifteen minutes and didn't hear anything, so I made my way back to the house.

The next day I left to go visit a friend. When I came back my grandfather told me that there was a corpse lying outside and asked me if I would take care of it for him. I went outside, and I found a skull, just a skull. It looked almost perfectly clean minus some dirt.

The way it was facing it was looking directly at the front door. I know my grandfather pretty well, and I know that he wouldn't try to play a joke or anything like that on me. Since then I've had some strange things happen.

I am still looking for answers, and some of the stories I've read on this page sound kind of similar to what I have experienced off and on. I live off of Highway 11 in Landrum, and I've been living here for about fifteen years.

Submitted by Jesse, Landrum, South Carolina

. . . .

41.
Small House With Full Basement
Huntsville, Arkansas

I lived on a farm about 3.5 miles from Huntsville, located in between the communities of Hindsville and Wesley up on a mountain. From the time I moved there around 1978 until I moved away in 1988 there were strange events that took place. The house was small but had a full basement. It had been built in the same location as an old farm house that had previously stood there and was torn down.

According to neighbors who had lived in this community, there had been a family living in the old farmhouse who had lost the mother who died shortly after her baby was born. There was also a guy who had turned his wagon over and was killed on the road that ran past the house. The road is closed off now and only a private drive to the house. The house is about a mile from a cemetery. There was an old well and an old fireplace that had rocks with dates carved in them for 1884.

I would be down in the basement painting pictures and would hear what sounded like someone opening the living room door, entering the living room up above me, and walking all the way down the hallway off the kitchen to the back bedrooms. I would get up and go upstairs thinking my parents had returned. There was

86

no one there, and my parents were not home at the time. It sounded like a man's stride when you heard the walking.

I finally told my mom about it, and she said it had happened to her as well. After I moved away my mom said she had been in one of the back bedrooms with my daughter she was babysitting, who was about two years old when the bedroom door just opened on its own. She reclosed it thinking the wind had done it somehow even though the windows weren't open, and there were no drafts.

My mom said it happened again one time while she was in the master bathroom. After she had gotten out of shower she got dressed and went to open the bathroom door. It was like someone was holding the knob to keep her from turning it. No one was home but her at the time. Neither of us ever felt threatened, but we felt there was something going on there at times.

Submitted by Anonymous, Huntsville, Arkansas

. . . .

42.
Old Nursing Home
Mountain Home, Arkansas

The old nursing home on Hwy 5 north of Mountain Hone known as Auburn Hills is very haunted. I took a group of curious people who wanted to do a ghost hunt to the old building. It was recently sold, and I obtained permission from the owner to do a ghost hunt there. Now being a believable skeptic as I call myself meaning I do believe but I try to debunk everything, I did not get the full effect of the hunt until a few days later when I was reviewing the video footage.

Out of the seven of us with cameras and audio recorders spirit boxes and a K2 meter, I saw several black masses and a ton of sprit orbs. We had two women there, one was a sensitive and the other a newly discovered medium, which means she recently discovered her ability and was still learning. They had both told me of seeing things right in front of me which I just shrugged off with a doubt and statement of "I don't see anything".

I happened to catch a lot of orbs which most appeared to be trying to hide or get away from me, and a few others were very curious about the spirit box and talking with the younger females that had the spirit box. The masses were what really got to me. To see a black mist just float through a wall was definitely interesting to say the least. I am hoping we will be able to get permission to go back soon, but from what the owner said the building has been sold and will be changing hands soon.

Submitted by John, Mountain Home, Arkansas

. . . .

43.

A House on 7th Street
Fernandina Beach, Florida

I lived in Fernandina from the beginning of 1968 until 1970. My husband (then) was with a company that moved us about on different projects. We rented a place on 7th Street close to town. My nextdoor neighbor owned it and was a retired school teacher. She showed me a map or possibly a copy of a map that showed the town of Fernandina in 1865. It had the houses drawn instead of just the streets. She said her house and mine had a walkway attaching the upstairs of both houses at that time and was a girls' school. It showed stables in the back. She said the horses and carriages would go under the walkway to get to the back where the stables were.

There were many things that happened in that house that I thought were odd or creepy, but I never really said too much about it. I believe my husband, being somewhat older than I am, thought something was going on, but didn't want to scare me. One night I awoke in the middle of the night hearing a noise. When I opened my eyes, from our bedroom I could see through the dining room into the kitchen where it appeared a dim light illuminated the entire room. I got up and walked to the kitchen door, and the ceiling light was barely burning like a candle. The noise was coming from the washing machine across the room. It seemed that it was trying to start up but did not have enough energy. I went back and woke my husband. He walked to the kitchen with me. The light was still burning, and the washing machine was still trying to start up. He walked over to the washing machine and turned the dial on and off with no results. When we flipped the light switch on and off, it just kept burning. It would not turn off.

About that time I looked up the long hallway, and lights were burning brightly in our living room. We had two lamps only in there. We walked up to the living room, and the lamps would not turn off. I have wished in hindsight that I would have pulled the plug just to see what would happen but did not think of it at that time. This lasted about twenty to thirty minutes without letup. I asked my neighbor the next day if her lights came on during the night, and she looked at me rather oddly and said "no". The phone would ring at exactly 10:45 many nights. When I would answer, all I would hear is static noise. No one ever said anything. I had a lighted analog clock beside my bed, and I could see the time clearly anytime I awoke.

I woke up one night and had a fear come over me that someone was standing right next to my bed over me. I could not see my clock at all. The black image slowly faded to where it was gone, and I could see my clock. My daughter was a year old while we lived there. We purchased a house a street over sometime after that. It was also old, but we had no incidents of anything like this while living there. When my daughter was three, we moved to Georgia. She had a very strong ability to tell you things that would happen before they happened. It became an everyday occurrence. We asked the church to pray for her about this. They said it could be used by God or the evil one. She did it one time since that time a few months later but has not since. I have wondered if it had anything to do with that house.

Submitted by Faye, Fernandina Beach, Florida

. . . .

44.
No One Saw Her
Saint Augustine, Florida

I took the family to St. Augustine Beach just right off the A Street Beach access, so they could have fun while I tuned my CB radio. There were no cars for miles being 1/22/2019. It was between 5:30 p.m. and 6 p.m. I was parked as far as one could get to the dunes as the sign permitted. I was fiddling with the antenna and SWR meter.

As I was outside adding washers to my 102" steel whip antenna, I looked to my left towards the sand dunes and was surprised to find a woman in a long black lacey dress thirty feet from me. She kneeled down on the dunes with her face away from me. I figured "oh great someone illegally walking on the protected dunes".

Behind my Jeep Wrangler to my right I saw a man and a woman next to the plastic barrel trash can reading the sign that said no vehicles past this point due to the conservation area. I turned back to my left to see if the woman was still walking on the dunes. She had disappeared, and I did not see or hear her go anywhere. There was no way she could have left the spot without me seeing as the visibility was still good. My wife never saw the woman I described, and neither did the couple in jackets that pulled my attention away in the first place. There weren't even any fresh footprints from where the woman had been.

Submitted by Travis, Saint Augustine, Florida

. . . .

45.
Rush of Air
Olive Branch, Mississippi

I live in the Vineyard Apartments in Olive Branch. My husband, our kids, and I just moved here from Lyon, MS. One day my husband and I were standing in our daughter's room folding clothes. My husband was talking to me, then stopped, and looked in to the hallway. I didn't pay much attention when he walked out because I thought he was just checking on the kids. When he came back in, he explained to me that he swore he saw someone walk from the back bedroom and up the hallway towards the kitchen. He said from what he thought he saw, it looked like an elderly woman. We just shrugged it off thinking it was just him needing sleep. (He is a truck driver.)

A couple of nights later I was standing in the hall bathroom doing my makeup. My five-month-old was sleeping in his bed, and my daughter was beside me playing with my brushes. My husband was gone on the truck. I noticed something looking like a black shadow go by into my daughter's room. I know I saw it because I even ran in there to see if my husband might have got home and was in there for some reason. No one was in there.

The following morning as I was walking out of the bedroom to get my son's bottle, something ran into my daughter's bedroom again. This time I felt a rush of air like something had run past me. I don't know if I was just seeing stuff, but it did freak me out a little. I used to be on a paranormal team, but when I got pregnant with my son I decided to quit for the sake of my babies.

Submitted by Jessica, Olive Branch, Mississippi

. . . .

46.

Cursed

Fort Payne, Alabama

I've lived in three separate places in Fort Payne, all with different experience. I'm very sensitive to the spirit world and pick up on things very easy. This first apartment my family and I moved in to were the apartments back behind Auto Zone. From the moment we moved in I would hear my name being called out around 3:00 a.m. That's how it started. For a few weeks I would hear it every night.

After a while I started seeing a black figure about nine feet tall. It was pitch black, but you could see through it. It was more like a mist. I started seeing it about 3:00 a.m. every night. It seemed like 3:00 a.m. was when everything would happen, but then it became all day and everyday. It didn't matter what time it was. When I would see it I wouldn't be able to move or scream. I would just be frozen. It would always attempt to harm me. I would come out of this frozen state with hand prints around my neck that were so large; it wrapped around my entire neck with fingers overlapping one another marks on my body.

After years of living there we moved. The next house was next to the old high school which was a recreational center while we lived there. Every day I would hear someone walking upstairs. It sounded like boots with spurs on the back. It would walk all the way down the stairs, but I never saw it. I never felt fear from it. My kids would call him Jimmy.

Now we live over by the fair grounds, and whatever is in this house isn't good. I will see a black shadow stand or sitting next to me, but when I look over it is gone. I have horrible dreams almost every night. It doesn't stop. Late at night it is at its most active. I work third shift, so I am always up at night around 7:00 p.m. to 9:00 a.m. You get a feeling of someone always watching you like whatever this is wants you to be negative all the time. I'm not from this area, and after doing some research on this land. I've came to the conclusion this land is soaked in blood. This land is cursed.

Submitted by Kass, Fort Payne, Alabama

. . . .

47.
Strong Stale Cigarette Smell
Mount Dora, Florida

My parents were renting a house on Harbour Drive, and everything seemed wrong from the beginning. Lights would flicker; doors would open; things would move, and honestly everyone in that house didn't think much of it. That was until I announced I bought a home the next town over, and my parents were moving out of Harbour Drive to live there. The spirit was not happy at all. It began to make loud thumping in the master bedroom and opening and shutting the door repeatedly.

My parents didn't believe in ghosts or spirits, but just a few nights before they left it made them believers. One night one of my parents was fast asleep, and the spirit yanked his arm so hard it dragged him across the bed. Then about three nights later, he went to go to sleep, and the headboard began to shake violently. He tried to do the same, but the bed wouldn't move an inch. With the many encounters that my family endured there, the one thing that would happen right before the spirit did anything was that there was a strong stale cigarette smell. I'm just happy they are out of there now.

Submitted by Noname, Mount Dora, Florida

. . . .

48.

Vanished

Okeechobee, Florida

Okeechobee is filled with haunted sightings and even haunted places. I lived in this town for over 18 years, and I had some scary experiences. Otter Creek is a place to start, but I never knew what was in that house, but it was evil and dangerous. I was only eight years old when I was in my room one night. I was always scared of my room, so I would stay up staring at my closet for hours because I knew there was a presence there.

It scared me to death when I heard a frightening sound of something being thrown across the room, and I tried to run out of the room. I was abruptly stopped by two red eyes right in my face. I remember not doing anything but stare at the glowing red eyes. The next few moments were hard to remember because I believed I went into shock, and I passed out. After that night I would sleep in my living room because I was so terrified of that room. I would only play in there in the daytime because of those red eyes.

At night it would be hard to sleep because of the ghosts. My forearm would be sometimes scratched, or I would feel something touching and trailing their fingertips up and down my arms. Too many experiences happened at that house. When we finally left that place I remember a woman, a man, and a little girl at the steps pointing at our truck as we drove away. I watched them until I couldn't see them anymore.

My grandmother's house is filled with ghosts, including my nephew and grandfather who passed away. My Granny Lottie would explain several experiences of running through the house or even seeing apparitions in the house. She even had experiences of her husband and my nephew standing in front of her bed staring at her as if they were visiting. I've always felt things there. My uncle's room is haunted. The whole place is haunted!

To continue this I believe a tall figure has been following me, but I don't know anyone close who is this tall. I've heard growling and shadows in the morning and walking around at night. The presence of this "tall man" has been around for a long time. I believe he or it followed me from Otter Creek. I didn't look up information because I was too scared to find out who these apparitions arc.

Another experience was me and my mother at the beginning of 2018 at a fast-food place by the creek that leads to the lake, Taylor Creek I assume. Well I was eating and talking to her, and a boat was coming towards us to pass under the bridge. I was occasionally looking at the boat and the two men and women in the boat. I couldn't see the boat because of a large bush and a palm tree that cover that big enough part of the river. However, you can look to the left and see the river just before the bridge. I was waiting to see the boat reappear, but it didn't.

I asked my mother if she saw a boat, and she said yes. We threw away our trash and went over the bridge to find no boat, and I literally was shocked because I saw a damn boat, but it vanished! My mother and I talked constantly about it because we didn't know what to think. She even looked up to see if there were any boat accidents, and there are plenty of reports. Okeechobee is quite haunted, and I'll always be ready to explore other places here.

Submitted by Katherine, Okeechobee, Florida

. . . .

49.
It Didn't Want Us To Leave
Atkins, Arkansas

I moved into my very first home in the older side of Atkins. I was very excited to start a life with my partner, soon to be married. Everything was fine for a little while, but then we started hearing things like thumps in the house at night. Then it progressed to doors opening or closing on their own. We would hear music that sounded like old fashioned music that was played when there was no talking on TV, just the music. We started having things disappear and reappear in other rooms or never seeing the item again. The locked doors would be opened. The dishwasher would start washing on its own.

We started the research to get any information on what happened there. Several people in the area already knew about the houses and its stories, so that explained why we got a lot of looks when we moved in. Everyone knew but us. After nine to ten months living in the house we decided to put it on the market. It sold within a few days which was a huge relief.

I came over one day while we were moving our things out to get things we had left. I went to use the bathroom. No one was there, so I just shut the door; I didn't lock it. When I tried to leave the bathroom I wasn't able to get the door to open. I turned the knob and the lock, and I was pushing on the door. It wouldn't budge. It was as if something was on the other side holding me in. It continued for a couple of minutes. Then I was able to get the door to open. At that moment I had never been so scared in my life. I left everything that I was going to bring with me, and I never went back in the house. I refused to go back in. Whatever was in that house didn't want me to leave.

Submitted by Haley, Atkins, Arkansas

. . . .

50.
Feel The Vibration
Marietta, Georgia

In late June 2009 my daughter came from out of state for a visit. I took her to see the local sights of Cobb County. We visited the museum in Marietta located at the Kennesaw House adjacent to the railroad tracks. We were standing in the room in what I believe was the northwest corner of the building when my daughter told me the building was vibrating. I looked at her kind of funny when she said that, and she said "daddy take off your shoes, and you can feel it."

We were the only ones in the room, so I took of my shoes and could feel that there was clearly a vibration in the floor. The vibration was very strong. I could apparently not feel it when I had my shoes on, but my daughter was wearing lighter women's shoes and could pick up on it. I tried to figure it out but could come up with no explanation. We were at the museum for a while afterwards, but no train came down the track which would account for the vibration. All I can say for sure is that the floor was clearly vibrating.

Submitted by Ted, Marietta, Georgia

. . . .

51.
A Lot Of History
Fort Benning, Georgia

I lived in Davis in 2011. I heard tapping on the window in my bedroom, and so did my kids. The water in the kitchen turned on by itself before. My hallway door that closed off the main part of the house from the hall and bedrooms used to open and close by itself all the time. I had strange thumping and scratching noises that came from the shed in the carport. Things came up missing. I heard footsteps down the hall. I would wake up in the middle of the night to the living room TV blaring full blast from the living room, and all the lights would be on after I had turned off everything. There was no timer on the TV.

One night I was in the living room, and the door to the carport opened and closed. I went to see, and no one was there inside or out, and the chain to the door was swinging. My husband had a heavy ball hitch from his truck that had been on the top of my fridge for months, and all the kids were asleep. Then my husband and I heard a loud bang from the kitchen. We went to look and the ball hitch was lying in the middle of the kitchen floor, and no one was even near the kitchen or the fridge.

My neighbor was outside one night and saw a little boy with a backpack in my driveway trying to open my carport door. Then he disappeared. My dog refused to go in the hall that ran to the front door and would not go in the other hall where the large pantry closet was. She yelped once when she did. She would go anywhere else in the house. My home definitely had activity, and I never believed in that stuff until I lived there.

I still stand by what I saw. It was not imagined, and I felt eerie when I would go down the hall alone. I always felt like someone was in my room with me. The very first occurrence was when we first moved in, and my pictures in my bedroom would be on my floor for no reason. This only happened like twice, but they were small, light, and not breakable, so I didn't think anything.

My oldest swore that whatever was there talked to her and would wake her up. My neighbor was over one night when the hall door was opening and closing. No one was in the hall. Everyone was in the living room. She asked whatever it was to knock it off. Then we all heard water running out of nowhere. I went to find the water dribbling in my kitchen sink. No one was in there either. I think Fort Benning has a lot of history, and that there is activity everywhere.

Submitted by Anonymous, Fort Benning, Georgia

. . . .

52.
I Have Seen A Ghost
Gainesville, Georgia

I had a strange experience at a restaurant on Green Street in Gainesville, Georgia back in the mid 90s. I work for a local florist in Gainesville, and we would have deliveries to this restaurant every so often. It was dark and gloomy inside every time I went in, but one day we had a shower reception at the restaurant, so I had to deliver ten table arrangements to it. When I got there I was early, so I went in and had to look for an employee to see where they wanted me to put the flowers.

They were only a couple of employees in there. The lady told me to take them upstairs and put them on each table, so I carried the first box up, came down, got the rest of the flower arrangements, and took them upstairs to the room. When I was putting them on each table I had noticed three tables did not have tablecloths on them, so I started putting the others on tables. As I started putting one down, I caught a glimpse of a person to my left. As soon as I put it down, I turned to ask that person what should I do with the others since they were no tablecloths on them. To my surprise there was no one to be seen. It startled me.

The person was wearing a white smock and white chef hat. However, he was gone in a split of a second, and the door was closed. He could not leave that fast, so I went back downstairs and found the lady that I first talked to. I asked her about the tablecloths for the other tables and had mentioned to her that the guy employee that was upstairs in the white smock had left so fast that I did not have time to ask him about the other tablecloths. She said "what guy?" I said the guy in the white smock and white chef hat. Then she told me that no one was there but her and another employee, and they were in the office. She asked him if he knew if someone else was there, and he said no employees have come in yet.

That startled her, so she went through the entire restaurant and upstairs and did not see anyone. She told me that they have had other encounters with customers before mentioning about an employee that came to their table. They would ask for something, and he would never return back to them. So as of today I know that was a very strange encounter I had come across. Was it a ghost or real? That was an eerie feeling. To me, I think I have seen a ghost.

Submitted by Wade, Gainesville, Georgia

. . . .

53.
Lake Buckhorn Mystery
Temple, Georgia

I have not seen a ghost or shadow figure; however, I do have some interesting stories. Westlake View Drive is a trailer park on Bar J Road. Local residents will be familiar with it. We had a rather nice piece of property on Lake Buckhorn, and it was a large part of the mystery. First you need to know several Native American artifacts were found on our property line and on our creek banks, including several large arrow heads, a few small one, and a whole spear one time. Much more was discovered when Lake Buckhorn went down.

We found an old sunken bass boat from the 80s at the bottom of the lake as well as a snow globe. We found the doors to three different vehicles and also more arrowheads. Another strange thing is many of our neighbors' animals either disappeared or died. For a while it was considered normal on this street for animals to disappear, and many were found later but rarely alive. We had noticed our dogs barking towards the wood for hours on end at seemingly nothing.

I remember when I was eight our neighbor's black Lab Sheba vanished shortly after one of our puppies had its neck snapped. The next summer four of my cats went missing. This continued for a while. Another odd detail was the alarming number of strays this street had. Every summer the neighborhood would be crawling with strays. We had an infestation of rabid cats for a little while as well. The strays rarely lasted the summer, and the dog pound rarely visited our stretch, so it seemed most of the strays vanished as well.

I know vanishing animals doesn't seem like anything, but at such an alarming rate it has to mean something. I think it's connected in some way to the stuff we found in the lake.

There's a small track around a little fence in the baseball field and a small trail through the woods. On this trail is an old deserted house. There are a lot of stories around the town about this house. Well, it's more like a shack. One story that comes to mind though is the story of some demonic creature that lived within the walls of that worn down shack. Many claimed they saw it. Descriptions vary. However, in the most stories the creature has horns. I remember when we were in grade school, me and my friends would walk this trail. This house always gave of rather foreboding atmosphere like it would swallow us up if we got to close.

Shortly after moving out of West Lake View we moved to Lake View above what used to be Dollar General. An older man had lived there by the name of Edward. He had died of cancer three years prior.

Anyway, in one of the back rooms there was this rather large Chesterfield that belonged to Edward. It was a true antique and was absolutely beautiful. It was full mahogany, engraved, and it had a large mirror on top of it also. This dresser had a mind of its own. It opened and closed all night and caused us bodily harm on several occasions. One time my mom was dusting it, and it slammed shut on her finger.

On another occasion when me and my mom were arguing, the mirror from the top fell on top of her. Then on one final occasion I was running through the house at full speed when the door magically piped open and hit me right in the collar bone. From time to time several people also said they heard singing coming from inside the dresser. That's all for now folks. Sorry, it was a little long. I have plenty of other strange happenings to share more.

Submitted by Hecter, Temple, Georgia

. . . .

54.
Something Dark
Hattiesburg, Mississippi

I once lived in an apartment on North 29th Avenue from 2005 through 2007. The first time I opened the door there was a foul smell. My brother and I laughed it off saying it smelled like an old retirement building. I thought nothing of it. I had the carpet professionally cleaned and soon didn't smell that smell for a while. There were also different things about the apartment that seemed odd. The back door looked as if it had been kicked in or somehow knocked off the hinges, and no matter how clean I was there was a roach infestation in there.

During 2005 after Hurricane Katrina, I met my biological father. He was from the islands of Jamaica. I was excited about seeing him and offered him to stay the night or two, so we can get to know each other. My dad slept in the living room and was a light sleeper. One night he got up to use the restroom and said he noticed a dark shadow at my door as if it was waiting for the right time to come in. He told me to cover myself and pray for protection.

A few months passed, and I remember one night sleeping and was awaken out of my sleep. I slept on my stomach, so I tried to get up out of bed but could not move. Something was holding me down yet I could see nothing. I was sweating so hard and was in panic. I couldn't move at the time. Eventually I was freed. A few months later my girlfriend moved in with me. Everything seemed normal except that smell. Yet this time the smell was a little different. It smelled like rotten greens or old meat. I chunked it up to her breaking wind in her sleep. Until a few days later when she called me in a panic saying "I can't stay here anymore. Not when you're not here. Something was holding me down, and I couldn't move. " I had a chill, and I did eventually move.

I never did research, but I remember having a dream that the apartments were once abandoned after a violent crime happened there. I had that dream while living there. The final thing I will say about this apartment is there was a picture of an old man in a rocking chair. He had on a long black trench coat, and he would just stare. The creepy thing about that picture is his eyes would follow you, at least while we were in the apartment. The picture has now been moved to my mom's house, and it now looks normal. There was really something dark about the apartment. I still think about that place to this day.

Submitted by Anonymous, Hattiesburg, Mississippi

· ·

55.
Marching Towards The Cemetery
Andersonville, Georgia

I was on a day trip with family. As we were riding away from the prison area, (headed towards the cemetery) I saw a big cluster of period dressed men marching. My thought was "wow, they have reenactors here today!" We drove past them to get a good look and then turned around to pass them again. They were headed towards the cemetery. They seemed very "in character" because none of them looked at us. Some of the car riders saw them. Some didn't. I thought it was odd because we were so close.

I needed to go to the restroom before going back by the cemetery, so we quickly stopped over at the museum building. While there I mentioned to someone on staff that I was glad I saw some reeanactors on my visit. She replied and told me that there weren't any there that day. I insisted I saw them. She said she needed to have a park employee find them to see what was going on because no one like that was supposed to be there that day.

I quickly went out to the car and had the driver drive to the cemetery and around the park to find them. The big group of men were nowhere to be found. I don't know how they were able to exit the area that quickly. In hindsight I remember how they seemed to be in their own world and unaware how close we were. I also kept remembering how the whole car party couldn't see them. The whole thing was odd.

Submitted by ParkWendy, Andersonville, Georgia

. . . .

56.
An Old Nursing Home
Vidalia, Georgia

As a child in the 80s my great grandmother would tell me and my cousins about a nursing home that she worked at when she was much younger. She would tell us that she saw ghosts on several occasions. At the time we thought she was just trying to scare us.

Fast forward to 1996, I was in my late teens and decided to move in with one of my best friends that had just moved in to a building that was being converted in to apartments. We were looking into the windows of the wing of the building that had not yet been renovated and saw old antique looking wheel chairs and hospital beds.

My friend's cousin and girlfriend moved in down the hall from our apartment. One night she and I were preparing dinner, and her cousin and his girlfriend came running down the hall beating on our door. They had been lying in bed watching TV when an elderly looking woman walked across their room and disappeared. We got them calmed down, and they went back to their apartment.

A week later they saw her again standing in their kitchen. Well, time went by. Neither I nor my roommate had seen anything. One night after maybe two months of living there I had fallen asleep on the couch waiting on my roommate to get off work. I woke up to an elderly woman standing in the living room staring at me. She turned and walked toward the door and disappeared. I was so scared to the point I couldn't scream. It was at that moment my young teenage mind finally put the pieces together.

This had formally been a nursing home, and this had been the one my great grandmother had always talked about! After I calmed myself down and got brave enough to open the door to go down the hall to tell my roommates cousins, I explained to them what the building used to be.

I went back there in 2016 with my then boyfriend now husband, and the wing we saw with all the very old medical equipment had still not been renovated, but the rest of the building is still being used as apartments. I wanted to talk to some of the residents but the building was locked from the outside. I will not tell its location, but I will say it's an old block style building with entrances on each side. It's one long hall with apartments on either side.

Submitted by Anonymous, Vidalia, Georgia

. . . .

57.
Two Inches From The Ceiling
Thomaston, Georgia

It was a long time ago, but there's a house on the corner of Cherokee and Kingston Roads where my childhood best friend used to live. He lived there with his parents and his little sister. We were best friends from first grade until about fourth. Once when we were both in third grade, we had a sleepover at his house. We were planning to pull an all-nighter, so we stockpiled all our junk food and all our sodas in his room. We got a bunch of movies, hooked up his PS2, and got started.

We had a fun night of video games and movies. Then it got late, so we started telling ghost stories, which as kids, we all remembered would make your legs go weak whether they were real or not. As we were telling these ghost stories, I and my friend heard noises coming from his kitchen and hallway.

We brushed it off like we weren't scared out of our minds. We made the excuse that it was just one of his cats causing a stir. Eventually the all-nighter ended around 1 o'clock. (We were lame kids.) Then we decided to go to bed.

My friend had tall ceilings and a bunk bed. I always would call the top bunk whenever I would come over, so I assumed my spot on the top bunk and dosed off. Then at about 3:00 am I was fast asleep. I woke up, and my nose was about two inches from his ceiling. Now keep in mind, his ceilings were crazy tall. Lying on my back in his bunk bed at the time, I could stick my legs and arms straight up and not touch the ceiling, so the fact that I woke up and was that close to the ceiling immediately freaked me out.

I started flailing my arms around and screaming. As soon as my friend got up scared because he heard me, he ran to turn on the light. When he hit the light switch, I fell back to the bed on the spot. I jumped down as quickly as possible and began excitedly explaining what had just happened.

My friend believed me because he saw it happening for just a brief moment before I fell back to the bed. We ran straight to his parents' bedroom and began to tell them the story of my late night floating. They laughed and brushed it off as a bad dream or something.

To this day that experience has stuck with me. I never went back in that house. I still kept in touch with my friend though. We still are in contact today. We are 18 now. I could still ask him about it, and it still sends shivers up our backs. I never did any research on the house or even attempted to learn more. All I wanted to do was forget the experience, but no matter where I go or what I do I can't get past it. Luckily, I haven't had any other experiences since then, but I think the one time was more than plenty enough for me.

Submitted by Anonymous, Thomaston, Georgia

. . . .

58.
The Judge's House
Rome, Georgia

After moving to the top of Turnbull Hill on the property site of an old Civil War Judge Waller T Turnbull, our family repeatedly encountered paranormal activity. The property was definitely a playground for spirit(s). One evening my daughter was in the upstairs master bathroom, fixing her makeup and hair. Since it was a Jack n Jill bathroom I was in there with her. She looked to her left and saw the apparition of a Civil War soldier staring at her. She stopped what she was doing and went quickly downstairs. The door to that room would slam, and there was running back and forth from that room upstairs to my daughter's room on the other end at night.

Every time we left home for several hours, we would set the alarm to the house. We would leave in our car from the house, and the alarm would go off and call the alarm company. The alarm company would then call Floyd Co Police Department, and they would follow up on the alarm company's call. This was happening repeatedly at $50 per alarm call, so we finally quit setting the alarm. The alarm company would always tell us the activity setting off the alarm would come from the upstairs bedroom. We didn't have anyone or any pets around to set the alarm off.

Finally, they asked if we had suspected paranormal activity.

In the entrance hall of this house I had hung a shelf and put a decorative candle holder and candle in it. One night during a thunderstorm I heard a thud on the floor. The candle in the candlestick was lying on the floor. I moved the shelf and put the candle stick in another room after that, and it happened again. We finally moved from Rome, and I gave the shelf candle holder and candle stick away before leaving our home. There was also an incident with a toy in my daughter's upstairs bedroom in which the toy would activate. I had to manually turn the toy off.

The house of this Civil War judge had burned to the ground before 1935. The fire ruins stayed in place until our home was built by another family. When we moved in all of this paranormal activity started happening around us. When asking the wife of the builder of this house if she had ever experienced such things when she lived there, she would repeatedly make me feel like my imagination was running away with me. I did some research and found out that a child George Turnbull had died in that fire. I was never able to put my fingers back on that information even thought I re-hunted for it several times.

Before I sign out I want to relate that a sweet perfume-like odor ran me out of the downstairs computer room.

I knew immediately it was the perfume of an old woman, and I quickly left the room. I never told anyone outside my family about the paranormal activity with the exception of the wife of the builder who had once lived there. I wanted to be able to sell this house, and I didn't want the paranormal experiences to hurt the sale of the house. We moved away two and a half years ago and sold it to a young family of four.

Submitted by J.C. Taylor, Rome, Georgia

. . . .

59.
Child Like Entity
Rome, Georgia

I was born and raised in Rome, and just about every home I have lived in I have had experiences in. I am more open to things than most people are, so I feel that spirits are drawn to it. I currently live in an old mill house on Riverside. It's a beautiful brick house with hardwood floors and a fenced in yard. When my boyfriend and I found this place we fell in love instantly. It was everything we were looking for and plenty of space for us and the kids.

Now my boyfriend would probably tell you that I am just crazy or imagining things, but he works nights and is never here when things happen. I noticed my kids would gravitate towards a corner in their room. They would wake up in the middle of the night staring at the corner. A week went by, and I finally turned the toy off. I couldn't stand hearing it at night. Things seemed to settle down for a minute because weeks went by with no incident.

Around Christmas I started noticing objects were being moved. Nothing big just little things. My tape for wrapping paper disappeared while I was wrapping gifts. I spent fifteen minutes searching all over the floor. When I finally gave up I found it sitting on my bookshelf. I started telling my boyfriend about all I had been experiencing, and he just dismissed me. In my mind I felt the energy was child like. Never did I feel scared or uneasy in the beginning. Everything seemed playful, if anything.

I remember the first time I felt absolutely terrified in my house. It was late one night, and I was lying on the couch watching TV. One of my feet was sticking out from under my blanket. I was starting to drift off when I felt something tap my foot three times. My first thought was one of my kids was up and wanting my attention, so I sat up and looked towards the end of my couch. When I saw nothing there my heart started beating out of my chest. I am serious. There wasn't anything there. My babies hadn't come in the room. It was just me. I remember lying back down telling myself it was okay. The fear I felt was from how real the touch felt.

The next time I felt scared was when I was lying in my bed. It was just another normal night. My heart started pounding. I closed my eyes and started counting, trying to breathe properly to slow the rapid heartbeat. When I heard the noise I felt every hair stand on end. It was like I had just been zapped with electricity. It sounded like somebody near my closet, but the sound had tone. It was like somebody had been right there, and they had cleared their throat. I refused to sleep in my bedroom for about a week. It got so bad I was scared to sleep.

This place is still my home, and I don't plan on moving. There hasn't been much activity in a while. It's still very child like to me, and my boyfriend still thinks I watch too much TV. Even though he has experienced similar things, he will brush them off and forget about them. It doesn't bother me. When my keys go missing I just ask that the spirit bring them back. My kids aren't affected negatively either. They have no problem playing in their room or sleeping in there.

Submitted by Shea, Rome, Georgia

. . . .

60.
Unwelcoming Vibe
Belleview, Florida

We moved into our house near the sports complex in 2013. It's an old home that belonged to my brother's grandparents. It has an efficiency that used to be his grandma's beauty shop. The house is bigger than anything I had lived in since an adult, so I was super excited to move up here from Sarasota. However, that changed the first night we had totally moved in.

The house has three bedrooms, two large rooms, and one smaller bedroom in the back. I remember my boyfriend had to work right away, so we didn't have our bed set up in the bedrooms yet. We were sleeping in the living room, but I kept wanting to set up my bedroom because again this place was bigger than I was used to, and I was really excited to get set up and established.

When my boyfriend would work nights, I would be afraid to go in my room. It just had this unwelcoming vibe that I noticed when it got dark. I brushed it off even though I felt things, but we were committed to a year lease, and nothing felt evil. I just stayed in the living room till my boyfriend got home, and we set up the room together. My daughter slept with me for a couple of weeks, I guess she felt it too, but I didn't want to scare her, so I acted normal.

Then we set up her room, and my daughter loved having her own bedroom since we had previously shared a room. She had a top bunk over her full size bed, and she would be up on the bunk just playing and enjoying herself in her own space with the bedroom door shut. Like I said, she would be enjoying her own space. One day about three to six months in, she ran in my room complaining of nightmares and a man who would be talking to her. She said it was an older man.

At first I chalked it up to an overactive imagination. She was 10 or 11 years old then. From then on she wanted the door to be cracked open and never shut. She wanted the hall light on and closet light on. She stole all the night lights out of the house.

I started to really believe she was being bothered, so I got a hold of somebody off of Facebook, and they came by. I pointed out the markings over every doorway, window, and closet. I asked my neighbors and anyone who might know the house or the previous occupants if there was something here, or maybe they were just really religious.

A medium lady came over, and before even entering the house she mentioned how someone in the home held onto negative. I can't remember if she said negative emotions or negative things. I assumed it was me since it hadn't been that long before that I'd gotten out of a negative relationship, and I thought maybe it were my negative feelings that I didn't know about. She had her sage, a little pot, and her feather. She walked to the house. When she came through the threshold of my daughter's bedroom, the flames rose, and she said "wow that's odd". This alarmed me, but I didn't mention much of it. It could have just got to a piece of the bundle that sparked to higher flame, I didn't know.

After she left I acted like everything was normal and that that medium lady had cleaned the house and my daughter had nothing to worry about. That lasted for about two or three months. Then my daughter started hearing things again. She would be coming into my room saying she had nightmares and still heard voices or exhaling.

My daughter is now 17 years old, and she has just told me she heard somebody breathe in her ear. I've come to the conclusion that she hears things and that I can feel things (A.K.A. Spirits).

I don't feel like there's anything evil in the house, or maybe it's not aggressive towards us. When my mom moved in in October of 2018 things have started escalating little bit. Unexplained things keep happening. I'm still not sure what to make of it. I'm not sure if it's my brother's grandparents or something we brought here from our previous place because I had other paranormal stuff happen to me since I was in middle school. I wish I could get a hold of the previous tenants to ask why they had the crosses above the windows, closets, and entries. I am determined to find out.

Submitted by Bobbie, Belleview, Florida

. . . .

61.
Last Room On The Left
Lake Charles, Louisiana

My daughter had a baby in 2014 at the Lake Charles Memorial Gauthier Campus. Her little boy ended up in the NICU, and she was technically released from the hospital before he was, but they allowed her to move into another room on the other side of the hospital which is usually for day surgery patients.

Most rooms were empty at that time, so she could remain at the hospital while he was in the NICU. Luckily she didn't remain there long. She was in the room less than 24 hours. I went to stay with her while her boyfriend left to get something to eat.

Her boyfriend hadn't been gone very long at all, and I saw something walk into the bathroom of the room yet the door to her room was closed. No one opened it to come in. I said "what was that?" She said "what did you see? Because I have been seeing something since they put me in this room." The ghost made itself well known for the short time we were in this room, and we were relieved that she didn't have to stay the night in there as her baby was released later that afternoon.

I often wonder if anyone else has seen this ghost or had experiences in this room. I don't remember the room number, but I do remember the room was on the north side of the small hospital, all the way to end of the hall. It was the last room on the left in the day surgery patient room area.

Submitted by CT, Lake Charles, Louisiana

. . . .